I N N O V A T I N G
DISCIPLESHIP

Four Paths to Real Discipleship Results

INNOVATING DISCIPLESHIP also available as a
Leadia.tv Experience by the title FLUX.

Will Mancini

VERSION 1.0

ISBN-13: 9781491039670
ISBN-10: 1491039671

ABOUT THE CHURCH UNIQUE
INTENTIONAL LEADER SERIES

The Series Originated Unexpectedly

Some things are found along the way, not calculated. Twelve years ago, my call into gospel ministry transitioned from pastoring in a local church to providing vision and strategy coaching for many churches. By God's grace I found unusual favor with a wide variety of pastors in different faith tribes and church models. I never planned to write, but eventually a passion for tool making would develop. Why? I observed firsthand how the right tool, at the right time, can change the trajectory of a church leader's calling. And it all started with the book Church Unique.

The Series is Not for Everyone

Please know that this series is not about minor improvements in your ministry. It's written with a higher aim—changed trajectory. Therefore it carries a bold voice and challenging ideas. It's not written to make you feel good or to entertain. It's not an aggregation of good-idea blog posts. In fact, it's not really written for most church leaders. It's written for the hungry-to-learn leader, the passionate dreamer and the disciplined doer. It's written for the intentional few.

The Series is a Unique Collection

I grew up with a dad who worked non-stop around the house. He bought only Craftsman tools. I can remember the trademark red color of the Philips screwdrivers and the signature-shape of the chrome wrenches. The reason he bought Craftsman was the lifetime guarantee. The reason I liked them is they felt different in my hand.

So how will the Intentional Leader Series look and feel different? We aim for these features:

- **High transferability through model-transcendent principles.** We are not creating tools to guide the strategy or tactics of one approach. Most books do this even without explicitly acknowledging it. Every book is applicable to any ministry model.

- **Immediate usability on the front line of ministry.** The tools have been refined in real, messy ministry. We will prioritize the application for your leadership huddle or staff meeting next week.

- **Clarity-first conviction.** This series connects to the foundational work in Church Unique; and each book, while able to stand on its own, will relate to and reference the fundamental tools like the Kingdom Concept and Vision Frame. The books will relate more like engine gears than like distant cousins.

- **To-the-point style.** These aren't gift books or lite e-books created for advertising purposes. We want to bring short reads with sharp insight. We want a tool you can read in an hour, but change your leadership forever.

- **Gospel confidence.** The only real power center for ministry is the Gospel and we are not ashamed of this reality! (Romans 1:16) Therefore, no growth technique or creative innovation or smart idea should diminish a Gospel-centered outlook on ministry. This series will remind the reader that Jesus is sovereignly building His church (Matthew 16:18).

I hope you enjoy the contents of the series as we strive to bring you tools that are transferable, usable, integrated and direct. More than this, I hope they challenge your thinking and make you a better leader in your time and your place. Please stay in touch at WillMancini.com.

THE INNOVATING DISCIPLESHIP BACKSTORY

This book is special to me because it answers one of the most important questions for leaders who have read Church Unique and diligently apply a Vision Frame in ministry.

"When do we change our strategy?"

Some aspects of ministry DNA and vision should never change. Everything else should. INNOVATING DISCIPLESHIP is about when to change. It will make complete sense even if you have never read the book Church Unique. But if you have, and you do lead with a Vision Frame, it will help you understand how and when to modify your mission measures and change your strategy.

That's why we put in the "four paths icon" at the end of the Vision Pathway. As you "live out" your vision, the next step is continuous innovation for the sake of your unchanging mission and timeless values.

Here is one little key to help guide the way. When you see the term "output results" you can think "mission measures." When you see the term "ministry model" you can substitute the "strategy" part of the frame.

May God bless you as you co-create the future with Him.

Rethink   Uncover   Talk Up   Go Ahead   Live Out   Innovate

Will **Mancini**

CONTENTS

DEDICATION

INNOVATING DISCIPLESHIP is dedicated to my lovely wife, Romina.
In my world of continuous change, she is a constant blessing.

Will **Mancini**

Will **Mancini**

INNOVATING
DISCIPLESHIP

Four Paths to Real Discipleship Results

Introduction

Fast Followers and Future Designers

Not being able, as times change, to change under the Holy Spirit is ugly.
- Francis Schaeffer

The big idea of INNOVATING DISCIPLESHIP is a simple whiteboard drawing. My hope is that it will help you achieve your wildest dreams for the mission of Jesus in the world.

If you are reading this you are most likely an early adopter. You know that change is important and you like it. Innovation is a word that motivates you. Innovation is fun.

You are a high definition leader. There are now more secondary screens in your life than children.

You are a high output leader. Multi-tasking and outsourcing are as basic to your existence as bread and water.

You are a high connection leader. You tweet at red lights. You "like" over breakfast. You read Seth Godin's daily post on your latest Applegadget.

And what about your ministry?

It's relevant and creative. My guess is that you serve in a multisite church (or just started something that will multi-try to multi-ply.) You digest new and dislike expected. You know what works. You think well on your feet. You care more about your community than the church down the street.

Honestly, you could pretty easily give a back-pocket talk on how to grow a church.

But as good as you are, you have a problem that you might not know about.

What is your probable problem?

Despite your strong gifts of leadership, most of your ministry is defined by fast-following and best-practicing.

Don't get me wrong. Fast-following works and best-practicing can grow a ministry. But I believe that God wants more for you and hundreds of other gifted leaders. I believe he wants us to exchange our fast-following for *future-designing*. I believe He wants us to trade best-practices for *better-experiments*. I believe real ministry innovation should happen with the frequency of the sunrise not a solar eclipse. In the end the mission of making disciples is at stake.

WAVE RIDING VS. WAVE MAKING

I've met more and more pastors who are tired of fast-following and best-practicing. They want to accomplish more with their short lives. They are through with riding the next wave and are ready to make waves instead. More of the same thing the same way just doesn't seem better.

Listen to Steve Andrews, the lead pastor of Kensington Community Church. "I planted my church, and God grew it big. We've done externally-focused, church planting, and multi-site, and we'll keep doing them. But there are not enough years left in my life to simply keep growing this thing bigger. I'm interested in something more viral. I'm interested in changing the conversation from 'where is our next one' to 'how do we release 250 of our members to take our city?'

What about you?

I believe the moment is here to re-examine our assumptions about discipleship. Who will bring it? Everyday pastors will—from missional dreamers and megachurch leaders to church planting geeks and multiplication freaks.

What about you?

You are a fast-follower but were you were destined for more?
You are a best-practicer, but are best-practices limiting you?
You are an able leader, but is there a true originator and ministry inventor inside of you?

WELCOME TO THE WORLD OF INNOVATING DISCIPLESHIP

This short read is intended to have a dual effect.

First, INNOVATING DISCIPLESHIP is an annoying alarm clock that will aggravate you (just a little). It's time to wake up to the photocopied patterns of ministry that are holding the mission of discipleship back. We can't have you sleeping in when a new day is dawning.

Second, INNOVATING DISCIPLESHIP is your Morpheus and he wants to free your mind. Or like the movie Limitless, this is the pill to provide access to dormant brain regions. It wants to create new synapses where ministry imagination expands and news ideas flash like 4th of July fireworks.

As we jump into INNOVATING DISCIPLESHIP, we will be working from a simple whiteboard drawing- one tool to equip you as God's co-creator. After all, he designed you to help design a better future.

If you are still interested, take a trip with me to discover the meaning of this little equation:

$$1+2+4+16 = \infty$$

one whiteboard drawing

defined by

two vision decisions

reveals

four paths to the future

that provide

sixteen super-questions

for

limitless ministry innovation

Chapter 1

Will **Mancini**

Chapter 1: Finding Your Vision Switch

[1 whiteboard drawing + 2 + 4 + 16 = ∞]

Do not quench your inspiration and your imagination,
do not become the slave of your model
- Vincent Van Gogh

Every once in while I find a new feature on my Mac or iPhone, because I discover a default switch or button that I didn't know existed. In fact, there is a specific definition for this:

[1]Default: a selection automatically used by a computer program in the absence of a choice made by the user

Many times it's no big deal, but sometimes I want to kick myself for missing out on some cool functionality. I didn't know the default switch even existed!

After a decade of daily conversations about vision with ministry teams, I have discovered a hidden vision switch with a default position in the minds of church leaders. But this default setting is not just about missing out on a nifty feature. It's about a fundamental mode of thinking that's limiting us.

Let me explain.

One question I always enjoy asking church leaders is "How do you want your church to be different two years from now?"

What kind of answers do I get?

---

[1] http://www.merriam-webster.com/dictionary/default

The most common two-word response is "more people." Of course that expresses itself in many forms:

- Increased worship
- More growth
- Higher attendance
- Additional services
- Reaching more people
- Reversing decline

Think about that for a minute. "How do you want your church to be different in two years?" Imagine the infinite number of answers possible to this question. For example, pastors could have responded with answers like:

- More desperate for Jesus
- More intimacy between husbands and wives
- More engaged in social justice and civic responsibilities
- More families having devotionals together
- More friendships with people far from God
- More students serving other students

But, for the most part, they don't give answers like this. Despite the rainbow variety of gospel-centered, life-transforming possibilities the most common answer is always, in one form or another, "More people."

Keep in mind that the one-dimensional answer of "more people" transcends an incredibly wide variety of church settings and leaders, from uptown to small town, mainline or online – from the newest staff newbie to the post-retired, hard-to-expire. Everyone wants "more people."

And "more people" is good. Jesus wants more people, too. And, yes, churches "should count people because people count."

But there's something important behind the answer of "more people." And that something reveals this default setting in the life of the everyday pastor. Church leaders are not just saying that want "more people." What they are really saying is...

"We want more of the same thing the same way."

Or to spell it out a little more...

"We want more of the same thing (people in attendance) the same way (with our existing worship and program offerings)."

Let's unpack what this means even further.

When a leader tells me that they want more people, they are usually NOT saying two things.

First, they are typically NOT asking for a different result. The result they were looking for yesterday was more attendance. The result they are looking for today is more attendance. And, without intervention, the result they will be looking for tomorrow is more attendance. That's the first way the hidden default switch works. **We don't naturally look for fundamentally new, different, or better results,** but more of the same of what we commonly measure.

Second, the leader is typically NOT asking for a different strategy or revised ministry model. They already have worship offerings and some arrangement of additional classes, groups and events. The second way the hidden default switch works is by reinforcing the assumption that the same results will come *in the same way.* **That is, the leader is not really exploring or imagining a fundamentally new or different or better model.**

So, the hidden vision switch reveals two default mindsets in most conversations about church vision:

Default Mindset #1: More attendance is our primary desired result.

Default Mindset #2: Our ministry model doesn't need to change.

Now let's examine a second definition for the word default:

> *A selection made usually automatically or without active consideration due to lack of a viable alternative*[2]

---

[2] merriam-webster

This definition exposes the liability of that darned hidden vision switch. What's at stake? Pastors make "automatic" decisions without "active consideration" of "viable alternatives."

So how do we open our mind's eye to consider new alternatives? That's what the rest of INNOVATING DISCIPLESHIP is about.

For now, we will end the chapter with this conclusion statement:

When a pastor thinks about a better future for the church, the default desire is more of the same thing (usually attendance) the same way (existing ministry model). We will call this "same thing – same way," thinking for short.

If we create a matrix of the four potential paths, you have the start of one simple whiteboard drawing. Think of it as an innovation matrix. Through this window, you'll see the four paths to better discipleship results.

Better Discipleship (Window:)
Four Paths to Real Discipleship Results
Designed for your Whiteboard

	SAME MODEL	NEW MODEL
NEW THING	**Path #3** New Thing – Same Way Thinking	**Path #4** New Thing – New Way Thinking
SAME THING	**Path #1** Same Thing – Same Way Thinking *This is your Vision Switch's Default Position*	**Path #2** Same Thing – New Way Thinking

Chapter 2

Chapter 2:
Scoreboard 101: Three Kinds of Results

[1 + 2 vision decisions + 4 + 16 = ∞]

Instead of counting Christians, we need to weigh them.
- Dallas Willard

The first of our two vision decisions is:

Decision #1: Is our vision to have more of the same results or some new result?

Identifying the default mindset in the last chapter brings us to the first huge barrier to innovation – lack of clarity about results. To the extent we are unclear about the results we want, innovation will either feel unnecessary or be driven by unanchored creativity.

I recently read a question posed by Mike Breen, former senior pastor and organic discipleship guru: "Why is all of our innovation in ministry about technology and not about discipleship?" That's a great question. His point is that conversations about innovation can easily revolve more around gadgets than changed hearts. It's easy to talk technology without connecting the dots to better outcomes in peoples' lives.

In order to equip you to answer Decision #1, let's provide some vocabulary and define some important points to keep you and your team crystal clear every day about results. Any result you can desire for your church will fit into three broad categories – input results, output results and impact results.

INPUT RESULTS

Input results in the church world focus on the number of people and dollars that "come into" the church. Input results are important. You don't have a church without them. It's also important to measure input results. You can't lead well without knowing them.

Common ways we talk about input results include the "ABC's" (Attendance, Buildings and Cash) or "nickels and noses" or "butts and bucks." Every week, thousands of churches across the land will print their input results on a worship bulletin or review them in the next elders meeting. Input results inform the functional dashboard of the North American church.

OUTPUT RESULTS

Output results refer to actual life-change outcomes that God intends for followers of Christ individually and together. Examples of output results include the quality of a believer's prayer life, the skillfulness in sharing the gospel, or the development of patience as one of the fruits of the Spirit.

There are hundreds of biblical phrases and concepts to capture the wonder of gospel-centered output results. Terms like "spiritual formation" and "transformed living," to "Christlikeness," and "full devotion to Christ." I have never met a church without some banner, slogan or mission that points to output results. Output language shapes the primary intent of all the pastors I have ever met.

While many Scriptures speak directly to the output results, three passages are noteworthy for how they bring clarity, direction, and specificity to our understanding of output results.

In the first passage, Matthew 22:37, an expert lawyer tries to trap Jesus in his words. The hope of this trickster is that the right question will trip a wrong response leaving Jesus tangled in technicalities. But our Savior masterfully eludes the verbal snare by cutting through the complexity of Jewish laws with a stunning simplicity. With a brilliant synthesis that we know as the Great Commandment, Jesus replies: "Love..." The text clarifies the singularity of love—loving God and loving neighbor—as the ultimate outcome of life in Christ.

The second passage points to the prime directive of the church. Although the Great Commission is articulated differently in all of the Gospels, the evangelical favorite is Matthew 28:18-20. In this passage, the output results of the church are preserved through the mandate to "make disciples." This mission is pervasive in two ways: it permeates the entire globe in geographic scope and it demands a full scope of obedience to "all that Jesus commanded." Jesus' disciples are to fill the entire planet and Jesus' teachings are to fill the entire disciple.

The third passage is Galatians 5:22, where nine amazing attributes, known as the fruits of the Spirit, expand our imagination as a beautiful picture of Christ-like character. In this classic "output verse" we see a wonderful specification of total transformation. We are not left with glittering generalities. The Spirit's desired end with us and in us is so clear and specific that its attraction and accountability is inescapable.

The output results of the church are black and white in Scripture. Most importantly, the living output that God requires of each one is satisfied by Jesus the One. That's good news! In other words, in our talk about "results" in general we must never allow legalism to slip in. Through the cross, Jesus' perfect life is credited to our account, so that our progress toward better "output" is centered and enabled in Him.

IMPACT RESULTS

Impact results capture the broader effect of the church in the surrounding city or community. Think of it as the positive difference that is made from the sum of believers influencing a region or pursuing a specific kind of social impact together. An example of an impact result would be lowering the number of homeless people or reducing the percent of teenage pregnancy or increasing the high-school graduation rate in an area.

The key to distinguishing impact results is that they are not a direct measure of the church's mission but a by-product, so to speak, of the mission's accomplishment. Using our example, we can be reminded that Jesus did not command his disciples to decrease teenage pregnancy in a particular geographic area. Therefore impact results may be the positive but the "not-necessarily-designed" results of good disciple-making.

For example, the mission of the Upward Sports is to "Introduce children to Jesus Christ by creating opportunities to serve through sports." When I asked Upward leader's to share their "best-of" stories, they recounted several impact results. For example, a father came to Christ while serving in Iraq. At the last minute before departing overseas, his son slipped an Upward Bible into his dad's military duffle bag. The dad found it, read it, and trusted Jesus with his life. Another story was told of recently separated parents who reconciled after a halftime devotion at their child's basketball game. While these results are wonderful moments to celebrate, they are not output results for Upward. The ministry does not exist to save dads or redeem marriages. These are broader impact results.

Other times, the impact results come with focused energy toward a specific vision. For example, Christ Fellowship in Miami launched a separate non-profit named "Caring for Miami." Among several social initiatives, they have rescued over one thousand babies from abortion through two women's centers. Again, this noble accomplishment represents an impact result, not an output result. Because the church has made and matured disciples (output), the presence of these disciples has saved the lives of unborn children in the city (impact).

Therefore, when we cast vision for specific kinds of impact beyond making disciples, or if we find the "salt and light" influence of our congregation noticeably changing the community, we call this an impact result.

If you want to have a whiteboard collaboration about results, here's how I like to draw it.

Three Types of Results

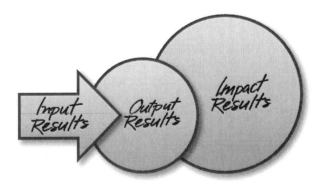

A tree is a useful analogy to relate input, output, and impact results. Let's imagine a Florida orange tree soaking in the sun and drinking in gallons of rainwater. We could actually measure exposure to light and absorption of water as input results. After all, you can't have healthy citrus without them. Output results reflect the total number of good oranges produced. Impact results are the happy faces and healthy bodies of little Joey and Suzi as they guzzle down fresh OJ with their scrambled eggs.

Three Types of Results

Organization	Input	Output	Impact
Orange Juice, Inc.	• Gallons of water • Days of sunlight	• Oranges per tree • Pounds per acre • Juiciness and sweetness	• Enjoyable breakfasts are more enjoyable • Vitamin C intake • More smiles for kids and moms
Upward Sports	• Kids attend sports league • Churches host leagues • Parents pay for participation	• Children hear the gospel • Children see Christ-inspired servanthood • Children trust in Jesus	• Increase in family member salvations • Lower divorce rate from participating families
Local Church	• Worship attendance • Weekly giving	• Engaged prayer life • Skillful at articulating the gospel • More patient	• Reduced homelessness • Saved lives of unborn babies

Our chapter conclusion statement is simple: **There are only three kinds of results: input, output and impact.**

Understanding these definitions will help us with Decision #1: Is our vision to have more of the same results or some new result?

Before we leave this question, let's consider one more dynamic that will help us make this vision decision.

Chapter 3

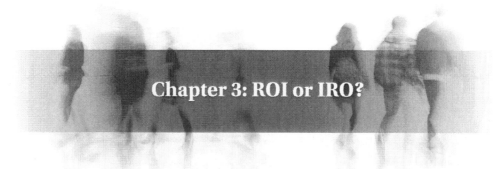

Chapter 3: ROI or IRO?

[1 + 2 vision decisions + 4 + 16 = ∞]

When I have heard of large congregations gathered together by the music of a fine choir, I have remembered that the same thing is done at the opera house and the music hall and I have felt no joy.
- Charles H. Spurgeon

Now that we have looked at three kinds of results, it's important to wrestle with a singular observation: **Despite the importance of input results, they do not provide a necessarily positive indicator of mission achievement.** More attendance and more giving don't necessarily mean more and stronger disciples.

The bottom line is that input results are not the church's bottom line. Disciples who obey Jesus are the church's only genuine product. Therefore churches can have fantastic input results and be mission impotent.

Every leader must decide where they will look to determine their success. I want to suggest two strategies for validation: ROI – Return on Investment or IRO – Input Results Only. Scripture reveals a God who expects a return on investment. But experience shows that too many leaders are satisfied with *input results only.*

INPUT RESULTS ONLY

Strong desire for, and careful attention to, input results are never the problem. The problem is when that's all we focus on. Over time with exclusive focus, input results become the pastor's *motivational bottom line.*

But a pastor will quickly push back. "Don't we focus on output results all of the time?" In a manner of speaking, yes. You see, pastors speak and teach and preach toward output results frequently. We traffic in loving God lingo and making disciples mantra. Our challenge then, more specifically, is that we allow generic output language to validate our intent while we use input data to *validate our success*.

Craig Groeschel dives into this dilemma in his book, IT: "If you ask most church leaders, "What's you ministry about?" they'll give you a predictable response: "Were about loving God and loving people" or, "We're about reaching up and reaching out." If you look at what the ministry is doing and measure it against their claims what you would find is often inconsistent."

The most important question to now address is "What drives our functional reliance on input results to validate mission success?" I believe there are eight key reasons.

1. **Input results are obvious.** Most preachers get up every week and immediately feel the fullness of "the house."

2. **Input results are tangible and therefore easy to measure.** It doesn't take much effort to get a headcount. And money is not only easy to count; our banks make us do it to make the weekly deposit.

3. **Input results pay the bills.** When I was a college student, I remember thinking, "It really doesn't matter how I spend my time, as long as my grades are good." The same is true at church. If more people and money are coming in, everyone in leadership including the pastor feels the day-by-day relief that, "all is good."

4. **Input results are legitimate output results in the business world.** Our elder boards and deacon teams are filled with lay leaders who sweat it out for high-expectation money outputs. Is it possible that the legitimate money metric of 9-5 also makes it onto the agenda for the evening church meeting?

---

[3] Groeschel, Craig. *It: How churches and leaders can get it and keep it.* Zondervan: Grand Rapids, 2008, pp. 42-43.

5. **Input results provide the basis for recognition among peers.** We have all been to the local pastors gathering where people either love or hate to discuss church attendance. Whether it actually comes up or not, it lives large on our conscious.

6. **Input results alone are more than adequate for highly visible recognition.** Have you noticed the list you have *not* seen from Outreach Magazine? How about the Top 100 Most Prayerful Congregations or the 100 Best Sending Churches in North America.

7. **Input results reinforce what the average church attender prefers as a definition of personal spiritual success.** Think about this vicious cycle for a minute. Most church attenders would actually prefer to define spiritual growth the easy way. Does God desire a radical transformation in my heart or can I enjoy great worship and teaching once a week and call it good? To the degree that a pastor is satisfied with just attendance and giving, people can live with lower standards of Christian maturity. Why would either the attender or the pastor break the comfortable, low-bar reciprocation?

8. **Input results enable less personal accountability for the leader.** This is not about ill motives per se, but more about a fluctuating energy level to stay disciplined with real outputs. There are stretches in my own leadership where a season of funk, or weeks of weariness leave me disinterested in real output results. All I really care about is whether the bills got paid!

These eight reasons give an IRO validation strategy a lot of horsepower. It's hard for input results to *not* be the motivational bottom line. The IRO posture is so deeply rooted in some of our churches that I have been tempted to loose heart. But, then I am reminded that Jesus will build his church. No consulting insight or fine persuasion can convince a leader not to focus solely on input results. It's a spiritual issue that the Holy Spirit can adequately handle.

Let's now drill down a little bit deeper on the most legit reason we get fixated defining success on the input side of the equation—inputs are just so dang easy to measure!

CAN WE REALLY MEASURE SPIRITUAL OUTPUTS?

Between 2004 and 2011, Willow Creek Community Church initiated a comprehensive spiritual growth survey with over 250,000 people from over 1,000 diverse congregations. Of their eight significant discoveries, the first is, "It is possible to measure spiritual growth.[4]"

I can't tell you how many conversations I've engaged where a team starts wrestling with the question, **"Can we really measure life-change?" The answer is yes.** Even though it is not as easy as measuring inputs, it is very doable! Keep in mind that before my consulting ministry I was a spiritual formation pastor. At heart, I am a mystic. So measurability does not imply that we can fully measure the holistic, expansive view of life in the way of Jesus.

Let's illustrate. Can you tell me how many people you could call at 2:00 a.m. if you really needed to talk? Sure you can, and that's one way to measure Christian community. Can you tell me on a scale of 1 to 5 how confident you are at articulating the gospel? Sure you can, and that's one way of measuring evangelistic readiness.

It really is that simple.

Let's walk through all the places a leadership team can get hung up on measuring the church's outputs.

The three common barriers to measuring outputs are:

The clarity barrier: The output results have never moved from intention to definition. Having clarity begins with a shared definition and articulation among leadership starting with the top 3-6 output results that the church is designed to produce. If outputs are unclear we always measure inputs. Imagine a leadership community of people who all know and share a passion for everyone in the church having at least five "2:00 a.m. friends."

The capture barrier: There is no current system to retrieve output information. Measuring spiritual outputs requires basic feedback processes and listening systems in the context of relationship. Tools might include questions, self-assessments, interviews, and surveys. Measuring

---

[4] Move, Greg L. Hawkins & Cally Parkinson, pg. 18.

nickels and noses requires almost nothing in comparison, so we settle for inputs. Imagine a bi-annual assessment conducted in small groups where people discuss and track progress in having "2:00 a.m. friends."

The comprehensiveness barrier: The impossibility of measuring spiritual progress *comprehensively* can keep us from measuring spiritual progress *truly*. It's easy to excuse ourselves from the task. But measuring output results doesn't require us to be God. And it doesn't require the perfect assessment. It does require a consistent, biblical and disciplined method to establish a baseline and track progress against it. Evaluating the number of "2:00 a.m. friends" in my life is not a complete picture of the commitment to Christian community, but it is a way to track true and meaningful progress.

Jim Collins speaks to the challenging but doable practice of tracking social sector outputs. "What if your outputs are inherently not measurable? The basic idea is still the same: separate inputs and outputs and hold yourself accountable to progress with outputs, even if those outputs defy measurement."

He even speaks to the problem of quantification, another reason so many church leaders pushback about being serious with outputs. "It doesn't really matter whether or not you can quantify your results. What matters is that you rigorously assemble evidence—quantitative or qualitative—to track your progress."

He illustrates how artistic excellence was tracked by the Cleveland Orchestra as a difficult output to quantify. For example, they monitored the emotional response of the audience by counting the number of standing ovations (output). They tracked invitations to festivals that correlate to an elite status (impact) and the likelihood that cab drivers would refer to the orchestra as a point of civic pride (impact).[5]

[5] Good to Great Social Sectors, Page 6-7

BACK TO VISION DECISION #1

Now that we have discussed three kinds of results and the dilemma of IRO thinking, I'm going to knock the ball into your court. **Decision #1: Is our vision to have more of the same results or some new result?**

I hope this question produces fruitful prayers and conversations. And remember: INNOVATING DISCIPLESHIP is written as a follow-up to my book, Church Unique, where I lay a broader foundation to this question with the Vision Frame.

Our chapter conclusion statement is: **Input results (attendance and giving) by themselves do not validate the accomplishment of the church's mission.**

Chapter 4

Chapter 4: Barriers to Ministry Design

[1 + 2 vision decisions + 4 + 16 = ∞]

The church world does not pay for research and development as pharmaceutical companies do when they are looking for new projects, or the government does to explore outer space. The most radical designers in the church world have always paid for their own design processes, either by being judged heretical by their contemporaries or by being unsuccessful for some period of time before their thoughts form something whole, systematic and useful.

- Linda Bergquist and Allan Karr

Now that we've covered **Decision #1** and the first huge barrier to innovation—lack of clarity about results—let's talk about the second.

Our second big barrier to innovation is a low competency in ministry design. For the average pastor the second vision decision is harder to think about than it should be.

Vision Decision #2: Is it better to use our existing ministry model or to introduce a change?

This question raises many others and really forces us to think. What really is our existing model? What are some of the kinds of changes we could make? Should we make small adjustments to our model or overhaul the entire thing?

I believe the challenge in tackling this question is not our ability as much as it is our mindset. So, let's cover some ministry model basics. My hope is to create some awareness and insight that will help you answer **Decision #2**. Are you ready for a crash course in ministry design?

Let's go.

The course begins by reminding you that many leaders can easily be more skillful in ministry design. What keeps leaders from practicing ministry design more naturally? Three mindset issues keep us stuck: category complexity, "program lock," and 2nd generation passion. Let's briefly define each one.

CATEGORY COMPLEXITY

In our current world of flux we are given countless ministry categories. These categories shape our reading, conferencing, and dialoging which in term shape or thinking and our ministry design.

The people who create our categories are:

- **Academics** who write about theology and often times don't have leadership experience. They give us important technical categories to think about within ecclesiology and missiology.
- **Passionate practitioners** who share their models. Each story fits a category or creates a new one. All I want is an exponentially sticky, totally deep, wholly hybrid, and missionally both/and church.
- **Researchers, writers, and blog aggregators** who give us even more categories – from a catalogue of best practices to the latest research to the latest five attributes of a thriving church.
- **Prophetic voices and rock star pastors** that motivate and mutilate. If these folks don't give us new category they will at least shake up the ones we thought we understood.

All of these people are gifts from God and agents of the church's constant reform.

But so many categories about how to do church create confusion and uncertainty. Many times the categories themselves are not accessible and actionable enough to innovate from "right where we are." Therefore, category complexity overloads us and paralyzes us. As a result, approaching the task of ministry design is more daunting.

PROGRAM LOCK

The second mindset issue is what I call "program lock." Program lock is the mental inability to see a different way of doing ministry because someone else made all of the design decisions in advance. Who would that be? The prior pastor, a denominational resource provider, the latest conference speaker, or a program-in-the-box maker. Let me clarify; a program is not a bad thing, but pastoring with program lock will get you stuck in an ever changing world.

My first car was a 1970 Olds Cutlass. I remember one day when I couldn't start it. Thankfully my dad knew the problem, which he identified as "vapor lock." The gasoline in my fuel line was turning to vapor, which in turn kept the liquid gasoline from flowing. With program lock a similar thing happens: a continuous stream of alternative improvement ideas is blocked from entering through the brains cells of the ministry leader. Year after year a leader keeps managing the same programs—the same "hows" of ministry—that were determined by a person in a different time and place.

Social scientists use the term "path dependence" to describe the same type of dynamic. The classic case study is the QWERTY keyboard. It was popularized in 1878, when the mechanical limitations of the typewriter played a role in determining key placement. Despite every technological advance since then, we still stay with the inferior solution because of our dependence on it.

2nd GENERATION PASSION

The third obstacle with ministry design competency is what I call "2nd generation passion." Every ministry model was originally designed to meet a need and solve a problem. What typically drives the creation or modification of a model is a deep and personal connection to some problem. When Bill Hybels designed a seeker model, he was emotionally connected to the problem that spiritual seekers had checked out on church as usual. When the leaders of Grainger Community Church launched their 2016 "Raising the Bar Vision" they were emotionally connected to the problem that a large attractional service can be a barrier to releasing and reproducing people to "be the church."

When a leader copies another ministry model, the emotional connection to the problem it solved doesn't automatically come with it. That's what I call 2nd generation passion. When a pastor is stuck in program lock, they are operating with 2nd generation passion. To whatever degree the "original pain" of a problem is missing, the drive and courage to shape new strategy will be missing.

Here is my brief prescription for each of these ministry design barriers:

- **Category Complexity:** Keep reading because INNOVATING DISCIPLESHIP will provide some simpler categories.
- **Program Lock:** Analyze your own "pathway dependence" by reviewing your history in ministry. Who made the decisions about the model you were leading at every chapter in your story?
- **2nd Generation Passion:** Prayerfully pay more attention to the needs of people right where God as placed you. Cultivate your holy discontent by listening to the voice of the Father as you stay immersed in culture. What drives you today? What originally drove the model you are using?

Our chapter conclusion statement is: **Thinking of new ways to design ministry is difficult because we have a truckload of ideas dumped on us (category complexity), we get stuck in an existing model for doing things (program lock), and we are not deeply in tune with the original problem that our models solve (2nd generation passion).**

Chapter 5

Will **Mancini**

Chapter 5:
Three Approaches to Church Strategy

[1 + 2 vision decisions + 4 + 16 = ∞]

Spiritual formation doesn't happen in a program at the church. It happens by living your life. We really need to stay away from creating programs as our goal. Programs have their place, but they must be subordinated to the spiritual life.
- Dallas Willard

In this next chapter we will continue to address **Vision Decision #2: Is it better to use our existing ministry model or to introduce a change?** First, we will focus on elements of ministry design. Then, we will provide a simple design "portal" to jumpstart your thinking as a future designer. With this perspective you can evaluate your current ministry and create an actionable blueprint for ministry model changes.

YOUR MINISTRY MODEL = PATTERN OF "ENGAGEMENTS"

Let's start by thinking of your church's ministry model as pattern of "engagements" that are designed to produce certain outcomes. Engagements include any array of activities you offer from worship to mission trips. They are what you promote each week in your worship guide and every day on your website. They include all of groups, classes, events and initiatives that a church can offer. They include programs at church or anywhere away from church, like a home-based life group or a community-based service initiative. If it's a place I can go or something I can do in the name of your church, it's an engagement.

SEVEN ELEMENTS IN EVERY ENGAGMENT

Now let's analyze this idea of an "engagement." Every engagement that your church offers has seven basic components; think of seven gears in the machine that make it work. The essence of ministry design is the ability to build and tweak these seven components to get better results. The seven elements of a ministry engagement are:

- **Purpose:** Why does this engagement exist and how does it relate to other engagements in order to achieve our results?
- **Rhythm:** What is the duration and frequency of the engagement?
- **Environment:** In what general environment does the engagement take place?
- **Relationships:** What kind of relational development is expected to happen?
- **Content:** What content is required in order to accomplish the purpose?
- **Leadership:** Who will lead and how will they provide leadership?
- **Tools:** What tools are required to help accomplish the purpose?

Seven Elements of a Ministry Engagement

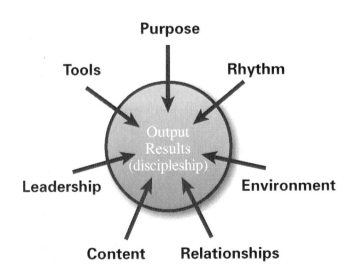

As you step into the role of a ministry designer, all seven of the elements will be important. But the first three alone provide important insight into your church's strategy and the ability to build output results into your ministry model.

Let's take a close look at the first three.

Engagement Purpose: Every engagement has a primary purpose. The most common purposes are worship, community, service, instruction, and conversion (I prefer the term conversion to "mission" or "evangelism"). While several overlapping functions may be present, it's helpful to define the overall purpose.

Engagement Rhythm: Every engagement has duration and frequency. Is it a 2-month process or a 2-year process? Will the engagement happen weekly, bi-weekly, or monthly? Less frequent engagements could occur quarterly or annually and more frequent engagements could happen daily. Rhythms in ministry (and life in general) are synced with the rhythms that God built into creation.

Environment: There are three environments for engagements. The first two environments are in the physical sphere. I call them "church space" and "life space." They work just like they sound. Some groups take place in dedicated church architecture and some don't—it's that simple. Technology has opened up an entirely new sphere—a virtual one. The ability to connect virtually has and continues to become a full-bodied expression of different of all of the different purposes—from worship online to digital missions.

THE THREE APPROACHES TO CHURCH STRATEGY

Last night I spent five hours with twelve leaders in a church vision process. The twelve people were made up of six pastoral staff and six lay leaders. They brought me in to help them design a better model of ministry. My greatest challenge in helping this group is quickly getting them to agree on "what is," "what could be," and then what "should be." How do you start? How do you bring all these very different perspectives together?

The most helpful approach I have ever used is the three approaches to church strategy.

The three approaches are basically determined by the first three (of the seven) design elements alone. Remember your ministry model is nothing more than a pattern of engagements. And the purpose, rhythm and environments for your engagements will determine your strategic approach.

The three approaches to church strategy are:
- **More is more**
- **Less is more**
- **To be is more**

Let's ask three simple questions to identify what kind of approach represents your church.

1) Rhythm question: How many weekly engagements do we expect of people?
2) Purpose question: What are purposes of the weekly engagements and how do they relate?
3) Environments question: Do these engagements take place in "church space" or "life space" or both?

Please don't underestimate the simplicity and power of these questions. How a church answers these questions reveals an "operational logic" and an underlying belief system about the nature of the church.

Let's walk through these approaches and use a simple diagram for each one.

MORE IS MORE

A more is more approach is seen in a church in which the basic operating assumption is that the more programs a church can offer in the "church space" the better. The hope is that more programs will attract more people and provide opportunities for spiritual growth.

Key attributes include:
- The picture of "membership success" assumes a 3+ weekly engagement rhythm.
- At least three of the engagements are designed to take place in "church space."
- The more engagements you offer, the less likely they are to meaningfully relate to each other or the mission.
- People choose which engagement to participate in with little guidance from the church other than advertising.

Implications of this approach include:
- Quality: The more engagement opportunities (programs) the church provides the lower the quality of each engagement.
- Results: With more engagements to manage it becomes more difficult to design any programs around a unified set of output results for discipleship.
- Assimilation: More options make it more difficult for people to take a next step with a new engagement.
- Time: The more time that is required in "church space" the more competition is felt with "life space."
- Culture: In a consumerist culture, a more is more model can easily reinforce consumer-like values in the name of "discipleship." Church may be perceived like a mall where programs are free.

More Is More Strategy

We picture the more is more strategy by placing the smaller "church space" circle in the larger "life space" circle. The smallest shapes represent the different purposes of a random menu of program offerings. The double line reflects the value of keeping church engagements in the "church space, which reinforces a distinction from life space.

LESS IS MORE

The less is more approach operates with the assumption that the church should provide a few high quality offerings. Whether or not these offerings take place in church space or life space is a variable. In addition, the church attempts to design these offerings so that they have a meaningful relationship to one another. Ideally, the program offerings are designed around a unified set of output (discipleship) results.

Key attributes include:
- The picture of "membership success" assumes a 2-3 weekly engagement rhythm.
- One to three of the engagements are designed to take place in "church space."
- The engagements are meaningful related to each other and to the mission.

Implications of this approach include:

- Quality: With less engagement opportunities (programs) the church provides higher quality programs.
- Results: With fewer programs to manage, it becomes easier to design around a unified set of output results.
- Assimilation: Fewer offerings make it easier for people take a next step. Fewer offerings make it easier for members to invite other to take a next step.
- Time: The less time that is required in "church space" the less that competition is felt with "life space."
- Culture: In a consumerist culture, the approach may attract people on the basis of quality. It may turn off churched people with a "more is more" preference.

Less Is More Strategy

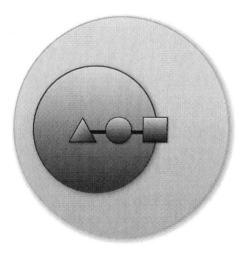

We picture the less is more strategy with a single line "church space" circle. The church offerings and programs are fewer—in this case three—and they are related. One of the engagements can take place in either church space or life space. This creates a "doorway" of sorts between the spaces. The distinction between church and life space is not as pronounced so the double line around the church space is removed.

TO BE IS MORE

The to be is more approach operates with the assumption that the church should provide as little needed in terms of weekly offerings in order to maximize output (discipleship) results in "life space." With a greater focus on "life space," each engagement is forced to have great clarity of purpose, and output (discipleship) results necessarily play a greater role in the church's identity. This strategy requires a stronger presence of leadership and tool development

Key attributes include:
- The picture of membership success assumes a 1-3 weekly engagement rhythm.
- One of the engagements is designed to take place in "church space." In some cases there is no church space so all engagements happen in "life space."

- Although engagements are more distributed in "life space," they are meaningfully related to the mission.

Implications of this approach include:
- Quality: The quality is determined entirely by leadership expectations and training, not by a church facility.
- Results: The purpose of each environment is usually clear. Unified output (discipleship) results are clear because they are the basis of an available offering in "life space."
- Assimilation: Next steps are driven more by relationships and a desire for spiritual growth, not typical forms of "church space" communication and recruitment.
- Time: There is little competition with "life space."
- Culture: In a consumerist culture, the approach dies unless people are serious about output (discipleship) results. Churched people who prefer "more is more" or "less is more" may not consider this approach legitimate or viable.

To Be Is More Strategy

We picture the less is more strategy with a dotted line "church space" circle as the "church space" is peripheral to the church's identity and mission in "life space." The church engagements are few—in this case three. A worship gathering happens in a "church space." But community and service happen exclusively in "life space."

APPLICATION OF THE THREE APPROACHES

Diagnosis – As you scan these three pictures, which approach describes your church's current strategy? Consider drawing a diagram for your church.

Understanding – Remember, we are focusing on these three strategy approaches to help "cleanup" some of the category complexity of ministry learning. We are not starting with terms like missional, attractional, deep or simple. We are also avoiding best-practice categories like multisite or sermon-based small groups or how to be a multi-ethnic church. These best practices may cause us to make decisions too fast (fast-following rather than future-designing).

Results – Looking at these three approaches to church strategy can help make connections between our ministry models and the results they are designed to produce.

Decision – Now you can better answer **Vision Decision #2: Is it better to use our existing ministry model or to introduce a change? What change would you introduce?**

Our chapter conclusion statement is: **Every model of ministry today can be summarized by three different approaches; these approaches create a useful portal for discussing ministry model design for better results.**

Chapter 6

Will **Mancini**

Chapter 6: Four Paths to the Future

[1 + 2 + 4 paths to the future + 16 = ∞]

Questions of implementation are of no consequence until the
vision can be imagined. The imagination must come before implementation.
Our culture is competent to implement
almost anything and to imagine almost nothing.
- Walter Brueggemann

In January 2010, the now deceased Steve Jobs released the revolutionary product we know as the iPad. Read the words used to describe the product in the introductory video:

- When something exceeds our ability to understand how it works, it sort of becomes magical
- It's hard to see how something so simple can be so capable
- It's going to change the way we do the things we do, every day
- I don't have to change myself to fit it; it fits me
- You get an order of magnitude more powerful
- We decided, "Let's redesign it all...let's redesign and reimagine and rebuild from the ground up..."

When I watched this introductory video I could only think of one thing, and it wasn't the iPad. All I could think of was the local church. The thought kept going through my mind, "What if people talked about the church this way?"

Reread the list, but this time thinking about your church.
Is there even room for a comparison of Apple's advancements to gospel-centered ministry? I believe so.

Listen to the linchpin strategy of Apple's success:

"It's built by our hardware team in concert with our software team and what that gives you is a level of performance that you can't get any other way. Apple is the one place that you can really do this. We build battery technology, we build chip technology and we build software and we bring all those things together in way that no one else can do it." [6]

Apple's success comes from a reimagined, ground-up design that leads to better integration around the desired results.

FROM THE SPIRIT OF APPLE TO THE HOLY SPIRIT

The big idea of INNOVATING DISCIPLESHIP is a simple whiteboard drawing. The purpose behind this drawing is that you would dream and deliver like Apple—reimagining, building from the ground-up, and integrating you ministry model for better results.

Now let's connect our one white board drawing and two vision decisions to reveal the four paths to the future.

We have laid the foundation with a discussion on results. When you think about the future of your ministry, what result is most important?

Decision #1: Is our vision to have more of the same results or some new result?

Your only answer is "same result" or "new result." Which is it for you?

We continued our conversation with ministry design. How do get past the category complexity of church ideas? How do we break free from the program lock? The answer will inform how we think about your ministry model, which will lead us to a second decision.

Vision Decision #2: Is it better to use our existing ministry model or to introduce a change?

---

[6] I captured this statement on the promo video for the original iPad at Apple.com. The video is no longer live due to product evolution.

Your only possible answers are either "same model" or "new model." Which is it for you?

When we get more specific with our initial whiteboard drawing we can see the four paths to better discipleship.

On the first path we MAXIMIZE the same model for the same results.
On the second path we ADAPT the existing model for the same results.
On the third path we INFUSE new results into an existing model.
On the fourth path we CREATE new results with a new model.

Better Discipleship Window:
Four Paths to Real Discipleship Results

	SAME MODEL	NEW MODEL
NEW RESULTS	**Infuse** Innovation brings new expectations and revitalized purpose to familiar ministry patterns. *DANGER – Unwillingness to modify the basic model can limit new results.*	**Create** Innovation enables completely new outcomes with new ministry designs. *DANGER – Creativity is a fun first step but implementing takes a lot of work.*
SAME RESULTS	**Maximize** No innovation is necessary to reach more people. *DANGER – Leaders may never see past the maximize "default switch" and get stuck.*	**Adapt** Innovation enhances the ministry relevance and extends ministry reach with model modifications. *DANGER - Leaders assume there will be output and impact results when input results increase.*

Let's walk through each of the four paths. As we do, I will provide questions and illustrations to stimulate your dreaming and kick-start your doing. We will cover the first path at the close of this chapter and then dedicate a separate chapter to each of the other three.

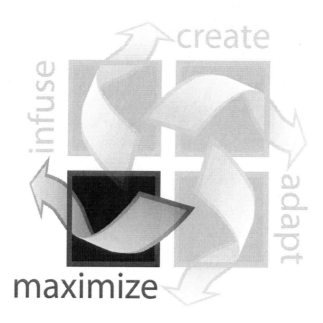

PATH #1 MAXIMIZE

While Path #1 is an important option for leadership, I didn't write this book to help you maximize your existing model. If there's flux in the world, then models must change in the world of church. Nevertheless, I will say a few things to put the other paths in context.

When you are getting great results with your model of ministry you don't want to change, the path to a better future is to maximize. You simply want to make the most of your model. Questions related to this path relate to **optimization, increase, strengthening** and **sharing.**

IF YOU WANT TO FOLLOW THE MAXIMIZE PATH, USE THESE FOUR MAXIMIZE SUPER-QUESTIONS.

1. *How can we optimize our existing model for more of the same results?* An example of optimization is adjusting service times for more efficient people-flow or providing a digital version of an existing leadership training manual.

2. *How can we increase the capacity of our model existing for more of the same results?* An example of increasing is adding a third identical service, building a larger sanctuary, providing additional egress/ingress on your facility, or continuing to duplicate campuses with an existing multisite strategy.

3. *How can we strengthen our existing model to ensure more of the same results?* An example of strengthening is training leaders and volunteers, or moving a staff from part-time to fulltime.

4. *To whom can we export (or share) our existing model in order to duplicate more of the same results?* An example of exporting is hosting a church conference to teach others how to build and manage your particular ministry model. Or it maybe creating a tool then sharing it.

Again, much could be said about this path to the better future. But it's simply not the place that most of us need to expand our thinking. So if you are getting great results with a great model, keep maximizing it. If not, keep reading.

Our section conclusion statement is: When envisioning the future we must think about both the results we want and the models we use, thus creating four paths to better discipleship. Innovation is not always necessary and you should maximize what you are currently doing if it's working.

Chapter 7

Chapter 7:
Path #2 - Innovation as Adapting

[1 + 2 + 4 + 16 super-questions = ∞]

*The how of ministry is influenced by the who, when and
where of culture.*
- Ed Stetzer, Warren Bird & Elmer Towns

When leaders are getting the results they want, ADAPTING is another path
to walk. In order to keep those results coming leaders recognize that staying
flexible with their ministry model is essential.

The ADAPT path brings us to a juicy conversation. In fact, I want to squeeze out twenty-eight question variations from four primary super-questions.

ADAPT will enable you to **enhance, accelerate, expand,** and **extend** the results you are currently getting by making tweaks and modifications to your ministry model. What kind of changes are we talking about?

There are at least seven potential ways to adapt the model that is already working. We will call these adapt-actions:

1. Apply technology in a new or different way
2. Add or increase something
3. Eliminate or decrease something
4. Combine or separate something
5. Reorder or reverse something
6. Customize something
7. Partner, merge or outsource with someone

IF YOU WANT TO FOLLOW THE ADAPT PATH, USE THESE FOUR ADAPT SUPER-QUESTIONS.

1. *How might we [adapt-action] our existing model to <u>enhance</u> our existing results?*

2. *How might we [adapt-action] our existing model to <u>accelerate</u> our existing results?*

3. *How might we [adapt-action] our existing model to <u>expand</u> our existing results?*

4. *How might we [adapt-action] our existing model to <u>extend</u> our existing results?*

We list our four super questions with a bracket that allows for the insertion of any of the seven adapt-actions. Check out how this formula results in **twenty-eight** variations that can start a brainstorming hurricane! The most important application of them is not reading them, but carving time to revisit them in a collaborative, brainstorming context. When's your next leadership retreat?

ILLUSTRATING THE ADAPT PATH

"Combining" to Enhance Personal Healing and Wholeness Results
Good Shepherd United Methodist Church, Charlotte, NC
Good Shepherd is a United Methodist church outside of Charlotte, NC (gsumc.org) pastored by Talbot Davis. This church has the gift of de-weirding the Holy Spirit. They combine the full expression of the Spirit's power with and robust biblical teaching. (How many pastors do you know who went to Princeton and have a gift of healing?) One ADAPT innovation they pursued was combining a monthly prayer and healing service with their regular weekend service. The *combination* led to *increased* time for prayer and healing (10 minutes) in every Sunday morning service including opportunities for laying on of hands and anointing with oil. The adaptation brought the value of personal healing and wholeness to over 1,600 people in worship rather than limiting it to a much smaller separate event.

"Customizing and Applying Technology" to Extend Leadership Development Results
Christ the King Community Church, Bellingham WA
On a recent trip to Africa, Pastor Dave Browning and other leaders of Christ The King Community Church in Bellingham, WA (www.ctkbellingham.com) kept hearing cell phones ring. Only it wasn't their phones. Browning and his team learned that the African pastors in his network of leaders were three times more likely to have cell phone service than Internet service. Upon learning this, CTK leaders repackaged their leadership training resources into text-sized messages, successfully training pastors to the other side of the world.

"Outsourcing" to Enhance Generosity Results
Christ Fellowship, McKinney, TX
Christ Fellowship in McKinney, TX is pastored by Bruce Miller. While there is a lot I could write about Bruce and this great church, one thing I admire about them is their egoless passion for Jesus. This lack of ego combined with a vision season of "simplifying to multiply" led them to eliminate Financial Peace University. Only, they didn't really eliminate it; they partnered with

a church that could do it better and told their people to take the program at the other church if they needed it. They were able to simultaneously enhance their generosity output results and take another step toward multiplication results.

"Reversing" to Accelerate Service Results and Membership Decision Results
Cathedral of Joy, Richland, WA

In a recent neighborhood conversation, the youth pastor at Cathedral of Joy in Richland, WA (www.cojchurch.com) was talking about an upcoming church trip to Central America to dig water wells. Upon hearing the story, the neighbor asked the youth pastor if he could go. But there was one "problem" – that neighbor was an Egyptian Muslim. He even came back to the youth pastor later to say that his sister in Chicago heard the story, and wanted to go, too! The situation is a real problem if you have to be a member of the church in order to go on a mission trip. But, Cathedral of Joy decided to reverse the typical pathway of "belong then serve" to enable people to serve with the church before an official membership process. Church leaders like this are thinking beyond their members, and using community engagement to connect them to Christ.

"Adding" to Expand Wisdom Results
Chris Saulnier, student pastor

Chris Saulnier is a student pastor who has had pen to paper in designing ministry environments. Of several new ideas he is rolling out this next fall, he is most excited about having dinners in homes in gender-based settings where 8-10 students interact with 3-4 seasoned church leaders.

INTERPRETING SOME OF OUR BEST PRACTICES

Many of our best practices in the North American church fit into this ADAPT category, including the multisite movement, and the simplicity emphasis. Note that the primary result that occurs with these best practices is increased attendance as an input result.

Multisite - "Using New Technology" to Extend Attendance Results

If you asked church leaders who embarked on a multisite adventure why they did it, the most common answer is "more people." (Our default position again.) Most multisites *add* technology to extend their attendance results (input) in another geographic area. The rapid spread of multisite was driven, in my opinion, by the opportunity to get more input results for a lower cost. "Bigger box" building got more expensive and technology enabled the extension of a gifted teacher to another location. I have worked with dozens of multisites and interviewed scores of others. Most pastors of growing multisite churches don't have a clear definition of their output (discipleship) results. Keep in mind, I am not challenging their intent to reach more people for Christ, I am just reporting that the motivational bottom line is more attendance. Are there ways to see multisite as a model for new results? Yes, but that is a different path.

The Simplicity Emphasis – "Eliminating" to Accelerate Attendance Results through Assimilation

Books like *Simple Church* (by Thom Rainer and Eric Geiger) and *Deliberate Simplicity* (by Dave Browning) reveal the benefits of getting simple. Churches are always looking for better ways to assimilate people into meaningful ministry. Most churches pursuing simplicity *eliminated programs* (less weekly engagements) to *accelerate attendance results* (input) with activities beyond worship. For example, a simplicity thrust would involve removing competing types of group "operating systems" like home groups, Sunday school and women's bible studies to emphasize just one kind of engagement. Even though more simplicity by itself doesn't bring a new result, many times it encourages a great awareness of output (discipleship) results.

Chapter 8

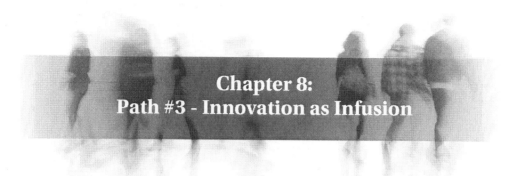

Chapter 8:
Path #3 - Innovation as Infusion

[1 + 2 + 4 + 16 super-questions = ∞]

Increasing levels of participation in these sets of [church] activities does NOT predict whether someone's becoming more of a disciple of Christ. It does not predict whether they love God or they love people more.
- Greg Hawkins and Cally Parkinson

When you are going after new discipleship results and you want to operate within the same basic ministry model, it's time to INFUSE. Your church will **activate, align, repurpose** or **remix** in order to follow the INFUSE path.

Many times INFUSING is useful when programs, especially in "church space" have lost a clear purpose or no longer have meaningful relationship to the mission or other programs. Every time I am with a church that has significant educational "church space," like Sunday school classrooms, we look for ways to infuse better results into architectural assets.

IF YOU WANT TO FOLLOW THE INFUSE PATH, USE THESE FOUR INFUSE SUPER-QUESTIONS.

1. *How might we _activate_ a totally new result in one part of our existing model?*

2. *How might we _align_ everything in our existing model toward a single new result?*

3. *How might we _repurpose_ one or more of the parts of our existing model for a new result?*

4. *What could be _remixed_ (combined and co-mingled) in our existing model that would enable a new result?*

ILLUSTRATING ACTIVATE

Chase Oaks Church, Dallas, TX

When you commit to a small group at Chase Oaks Church in Dallas, TX (www.chaseoaks.org) you also commit to serve the community - service is a part of the package schedule of their small groups. Every 4-6 weeks, instead of meeting for coffee and dessert, prayer and Bible Study, the church's group members are out in the community – serving the homeless, building a Habitat for Humanity home, helping a single mom and her kids, mentoring students – something that moves them out of the living room and into the street. The commitment is for one year; groups must serve an existing local non-profit agency that already has the connections and structures to link small group members with service opportunities. Simply put, Chase Oaks is activating a new result for community service through an already existing groups structure.

Broad Patterns of Activate: Many churches have a "church has left the building" emphasis on Sunday morning where people leave the church and plug into service projects. This illustrates activate because, it's really not a new ministry model. Essentially, the church is "borrowing" the pattern of weekly worship in "church space" to activate a different result together in "life space."

ILLUSTRATING ALIGN

Harvest Church, Billings, MT

Harvest Church in Billings, Montana (harvestweb.net) launched a season of generosity that they called the "90-day Tithe Challenge." In a completely aligned effort to cultivate stewardship and generosity, they involved all three strategic environments, all ages, and even created an online teaching tool to take people through generosity model that they created in-house. People could even get a refund on their tithe if they didn't experience God's blessing through the giving! In this case they didn't change their existing model, but infused a new result through a church-wide focus.

Calvary Baptist Church, Clearwater, FL

Calvary Baptist (calvarybaptist.org) in Clearwater, Florida has seen tremendous growth in the last 5-6 years under the leadership of Willy Rice. Several years ago, Willy was concerned that their desired result of "nurturing authentic relationships" would decline as worship numbers increased. So the entire church aligned around the result of belonging. Rather than using a pre-designed campaign they developed their own initiative called Belong 2.0 around their own mission measures of "Dynamic Life." In one year they increased involvement in Life Groups by 50%. In addition, they sustain what many churches can not – a vibrant on and off campus integrated Life Group model.

Broad Patterns of Align: A common picture of aligning is the classic capital campaign approach that many churches have conducted over the last several decades. The desired result is increased giving, typically being raised for building projects. The sense of importance and urgency created by the need for funds creates a church-wide "full court press." Worship services, all small groups and classes, all age-graded areas align around one highly visible goal.

ILLUSTRATING REPURPOSE

360Church, Sarasota FL

Steve McCoy started 360Church in Sarasota, Florida (the360church.com) with the big idea of "live large by keeping relationships small." They were disenfranchised with the typical small groups model that doesn't actualize an in-depth, life-on-life discipleship. But when it came to evangelism, the church relied on creative, servant-style, big events labeled as their "large circle" strategy. After a while Steve realized it wasn't working. The people at church were serving, but they weren't really investing in relationships through the service. People were "caring" without really caring with a "drive-by" approach.

So, Steve repurposed. They *were* getting results in small circles but not large circles. Therefore, he decreased the big event emphasis like blitzing malls with care packages, reverse-trick-or-treating and neighborhood block parties. Instead, he repurposed the small circles to include incarnational ministry (They call it "incar-tentional") and began repeatable service evangelism opportunities around relational investing. Some small circles embraced homeless children in the area and others have created tutoring teams for a nearby school.

Broad Patterns of Repurpose: Many churches with space for traditional Sunday school have watched all kinds of small groups ideas come and go. Most have tried to repurpose those environments from re-labeling to completing integrating new ways of creating community.

ILLUSTRATING REMIX

Saddleback Church, Lake Forest, CA

Saddleback's Celebrate Recovery program has become as ubiquitous as any program that I have seen. And it was started by an interesting remix story. The originator, Rick Warren, simply took content from the eight Beatitudes and combined them with the 12-step recovery process.

Bellevue Baptist, Memphis, TN

A creative volunteer leads a dynamic program at Bellevue Baptist in Memphis, TN (Bellevue.org) called Soulmate Live. How would you describe this initiative? Soulmate Live combines the features of a parent's night out ministry and an equipping class. Filled with live music, interactive table games, free snacks, coffee and cold drinks, insightful skits and entertaining video clips, it is a wonderful opportunity to meet other couples who desire a better relationship. Fifty percent of those who attend this remixed venue are not involved elsewhere in the church.

Chapter 9

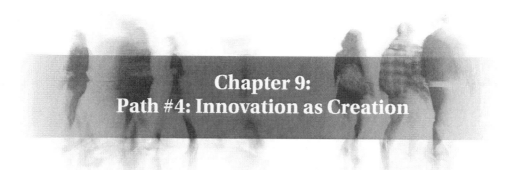

Chapter 9:
Path #4: Innovation as Creation

[1 whiteboard drawing + 2 vision decisions + 4 paths to the future + 16 super-questions = limitless ministry innovation]

No model is perfect and some are useful.
The hardest model to change is the one that works.
- Leadership Network, Leadership Community Maxims

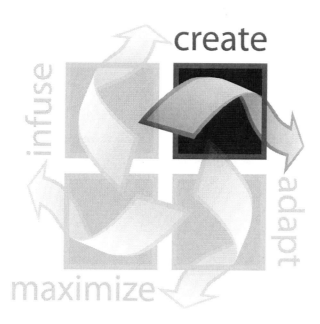

My friend Alan Hirsch has estimated that our best contemporary church models only reach forty percent of the population. That leaves sixty percent outside of the church's "cultural distance," no matter how relevant or externally focused the church might be. That's why one of the greatest reasons to create-innovate is to penetrate a new target group. As Craig Groeschel says, "If you want to reach people you're not currently reaching, you're going to have to do things that you aren't currently doing."

The CREATE path will take you in a completely new direction into uncharted and exciting adventures. Here, innovation enables completely new outcomes with new ministry designs as you generate, penetrate, incubate, or multiply. Are you ready?

IF YOU WANT TO TAKE THE CREATE PATH, USE THESE FOUR CREATE SUPER-QUESTIONS.

1. *How can we <u>generate</u> a new output (discipleship) result with our existing people with a new model?*

2. *What new group of people can we <u>penetrate</u> for the gospel that our existing model has never reached?*

3. *If we were forced to experiment with a new ministry based on a problem, a prompting or new possibility what would we <u>incubate</u>?*

4. *If the ability to <u>multiply</u> disciples, leaders, groups, campuses, or churches was not built into our existing model, how do we redesign it?*

ILLUSTRATING GENERATE

Oak Hills Church, San Antonio, TX

Oak Hills Church (oakhillschurch.com) has a dynamic duo ministry team with one of the greatest storytellers of our time, Max Lucado, and one of the greatest discipleship engineers of our time, Randy Frazee. During a three-year leadership transition complete with a vision overhaul, the church made the move from being "A Home for Every Heart" to "A Missional Heartbeat in Every Neighborhood." Oak Hills' leadership was ready to generate a major new result in ministry: recreating the presence of Christ in the "life space" sphere of the neighborhood. The result has huge implications not just for deepening community among believers, but integrated family discipleship and neighbor-to-neighbor evangelism. The fully expressed discipleship outputs of the church are built around "30 Big Ideas" divided into categories of think, act and be like Jesus.

The creation of this new model is the most dramatic "more is more" to "less is more" I have ever seen. It is built around a sophisticated set of rhythms in "life space" where disciples "go deeper" in the home, neighborhood and community.

- Daily rhythms at home as a family
- Weekly small group rhythms in homes with believers
- Monthly neighborhood-based gathering with believers
- Quarterly gatherings in a community area
- Weekly worship on "church space" at a campus

By design, the church's expectation of "success" does not necessitate time on "church space" other than worship. When a church as big as Oak Hills (over 6,000 in attendance) undertakes a church-wide model overhaul like this, the integration of a "new operating system" requires a tremendous amount of work.

ILLUSTRATING PENETRATE

"Church at My Place"

I was recently visiting with the leadership team of a church that has grown to around 5,000 in attendance in 13 years. The church on the Eastern side of the country currently meets in three locations. But the pastor has a dream that has been brewing for a while and is in the process of launching. The result they are looking for is a dramatic penetration of their community to reach people in the other sixty percent (the people who would rather be struck by lightning that come to church). I can't mention the name of the church because their plans have not yet been rolled out.

What new model of ministry are they creating? It's called "church at my place." While the concept of a home church is not new, their dream of sending a thousand people from a typical megachurch to host little worship services in their family room certainly is! They plan on equipping members with videos of the Sunday service and encouraging them to stay home so they can invite their neighbors to come over. (Can you imagine the push back from most pastors? "How will we count the people?" "How will we do giving?") But the focus is not on input results but output results. In this case making the gospel accessible by switching the worship engagement from a "church space" with hundreds of people to a "life space" with dozens.

Neartown Church, Houston, TX
On the opposite side of "large and dispersing" is "new and multiplying." Russell Cravens is church planter whose is penetrating a specific group – young busy dads moving back to the city. Neartown Church is officially nine months old with 130 in worship, the bulk of who have signed in blood as "mission partners." The strategy is a simple "to be is more" approach rooted in their value of "new relationships" as passionate and connected followers of Jesus. Russell leads with what he calls the "4x4" measure: start four new relationships every four months with people who don't know God.

ILLUSTRATING INCUBATE
Perimeter Church, Atlanta GA
Leaders at Atlanta's Perimeter Church encourage people to serve in an unusual place first: outside the walls of the church. Rather than making the perpetual pitch for ushers, greeters, and kids' ministry workers, staff member Drew Warner says that church leaders want Perimeter's members to live out their faith most in the "domains" where they live, work, and play.

Crossroads Community Church, Cincinnati, OH
Crossroads Community Church (www.crossroads.net) is leading four other churches and five non-profit agencies to build a one-stop social service mall called CityLink (www.citylinkcenter.org) that will offer housing, job assistance, and health care to needy families.

ViaChurch, In the Air and Everywhere
This incubate story is a close one to my heart. Over the last year I have been cultivating a core group of people interested in a different kind of church that would fully engage the virtual sphere for a particular target group- the highly mobile Christ follower. I call it ViaChurch.

The concept for ViaChurch came one day when I was acting like a complete jerk while traveling. Every service provider was making mistakes that day and as a result, I lost my sanctification. On the late night flight home I started daydreaming about better travel services. (The rental car industry is just waiting for a blue ocean innovator to step in.) Halfway through my flight the Holy Spirit smacked me around a bit. I repented. I realized that my expectations towards a utopic travel experience where compensating for what was missing in my heart. The Holy Spirit basically said, "You don't need a transformed environment to be happy when you travel, you need a transformed heart."

As soon as that occurred it was like the Holy Spirit stuck a Matrix-like plug in the back of my head and downloaded pages of ideas about ViaChurch. I realized that being a highly mobile Christ follower presented enormous challenges and opportunities and could be a strong basis for a targeted planting initiative. Some ideas include:

- The concept of a covenant network that would enable GPS location. Any traveler in the network could identity others at global transportation hubs.
- Gender-based microgroups could be facilitated virtually based on a travelers needs including prayer and accountability needs.
- Worship and small group content could be "pushed" through sophisticated settings based on the traveler's preferences.
- Application ranging from radical generosity to skillful gospel articulation could be nuanced for the traveler's opportunity.

If you're interested in being a part of the core, let me know. The question of incubate is meant to stir your holy discontent. The posture of incubate is one of risk-taking, probing, and adventure. Beta is better. Are you engaging in better experiments or just best practices? Do you play it too safe?

ILLUSTRATING MULTIPLY

Faithbridge UMC, Houston, TX
Faithbridge (faithbridge.org), pastored by Ken Werlein, is fast-growing Methodist church in North Houston that was planted in 1999. The hallmark of Faithbridge has been its authentic, true-to-life culture expressed through passionate service to the community. But, twelve years in and on the brink of doubling their worship capacity (the currently run 3,000 in attendance), Ken and his team are more fired-up about output results than input. Specifically, God laid on their heart the need to have stronger disciples, not just more disciples. They began to envision what a culture of multiplying

discipleship might look like. To mark the monumental shift they changed their mission from: "to make more and stronger disciples of Jesus Christ" to "making more and stronger disciples of Jesus Christ *who make* more and stronger disciples of Jesus Christ."

The lead team took an entire year to re-imagine the shift. The year culminated in four dedicated "design days" during which the next year of multiplication ramp-up and rollout was planned. New ministry design elements include:

- Re-articulating the definition of a stronger disciple, a 6-point output (discipleship) result
- Moving from a "free market" groups strategy to sermon-based small groups
- Creating a multiplication model within small groups based on triads (microgroups).
- Initiating staff and leadership triads so that church-wide roll-out is preceded by at least one year of experimentation, seeding and modeling
- A vision Sunday announcing the new mission and challenging everyone to take an online spiritual assessment

Community Christian Church, Chicagoland, IL
One of the future traveler flagships is Community Christian Church, led by Dave Ferguson. Started as a reproducing church, Community Christian Church (www.communitychristian.org) has a history of rapidly reproducing both campuses and churches. The leadership of CCC is building on their past success of reproducing "macro" and challenging their campus pastors, leaders, and people to reproduce "micro." While small groups have always had an outward evangelistic focus, they are now challenging all the small groups to be either a group on a mission or a group of missionaries. The group on a mission is brought together for a common case. The group of missionaries comes together so individual scan be held accountable for being on mission. When this shift is complete, it is the hope of the leadership of CCC to have the number of people who are engaged in mission equal to the average weekend celebration service attendance.

Emerging Patterns of Multiplication

Multiplying small for big results is not a new biblical concept, but its practice is getting new traction for the church in North America. Books that speak to this trend include *Church 3.0* by Neil Cole, *Exponential* by Dave Ferguson, *Viral Church* by Ed Stetzer and Warren Bird, and *Multiply* by Francis Chan. The growth of conferences like Exponential, Verge and Sentralized is another indicator.

Chapter 10

Chapter 10:
Essentials to Limitless Innovation

[1 + 2 + 4 +16 = limitless ministry innovation]

Flux isn't risky. Flux is what we're in for. Fortunately, flux is also what we were born for.
- Seth Godin

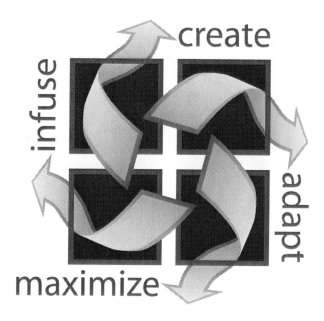

Whatever path to the future you choose, the process of innovation will require basic competencies in some areas not covered in this short piece. Therefore, I have assembled a top ten list of innovation books with summaries and links to related material.

As I continue to learn about innovation, here are the most essential practices that must be applied along any path.

Clarity: Innovation must be anchored in clarity first. Clarity isn't everything but it changes everything. Think about Jesus. No one was more clear about their origin, their mission and their destiny. Clarity is essential because the idea of innovation can take you easily off-course with spasms of creativity. Off-course for the church means off-identity and off-calling. I've created two tools to keep you creativity anchored- the Kingdom Concept and the Vision Frame. Remember, clarity is the least understood innovation essential among church leaders.

Margin: Ministry's overwhelming needs never stop coming at 120 mph. I have to remind myself all of the time that where there is no margin, there is no imagination. If you don't stop doing something, you'll never start doing something better. Margin is essential. It's the most neglected innovation essential to church staffs.

Heart: When you look at the business books on innovation, you get into technique very quickly. But the spiritual leaders must start with heart. The follower of Christ must study and embrace pain. What do I mean by that? All innovation is a solution to a prior problem and people won't care about you innovation until they emotionally connected to the problem. Heart is necessary. It's the most underappreciated essential for ministry leaders.

Team: Time and time again, the best ideas come from a collaborative engine. It's tempting not to involve others. We talk team but it's rare to find creative teamwork beyond worship planning meetings. What would it look like to involve more of your team more of the time for innovation's sake? For church leaders, leaning into team is the most inconvenient innovation essential.

Ongoing ministry innovation.

May your wildest dreams come true for the mission of Jesus in the world. As you walk these four paths, my prayer is that you would experience at least three dynamics of innovation. First is the heightened intention in everyday moments. Second is a value-add with major projects. And third, I hope you experience a breakthrough so startling that you can't believe that God let you work next to Him to design a better future through new discipleship practices.

APPENDIX

Groeschel, Craig. *It: How churches and leaders can get it and keep it.* Zondervan: Grand Rapids, 20080, pp. 42-43

Hawkins, Greg L. & Parkinson, Cally, Move, *What 1,000 Churches Reveal about Spiritual Growth*: Zondervan, 2011, pp.18

Collins, Jim, *Good to Great Social Sectors*, Jim Collins: 2005, pp. 6-7

Hirsh, Allan; Catchim, Tim, *The Permanent Revolution: Apostolic Imagination and Practice in the 21st Century Church*: Jossey-Bass, 2012

Will Mancini

Will Mancini wants you and your ministry to experience the benefits of stunning, God-given clarity. As a pastor turned vision coach, Will has worked with an unprecedented variety of churches from growing megachurches and missional communities, to mainline revitalization and church plants. He is the founder of Auxano, creator of VisionRoom.com and the author of Church Unique: How Missional Leaders Cast Vision and Create Movement.

Will lives in Houston, Texas with his wife Romina and three children, Jacob, Joel and Abigail. He loves to get out of Houston as much as possible for mountain biking and snowboarding. His pastoral experience includes leadership development responsibilities at Clear Creek Community Church and Faithbridge UMC. Both churches have experienced dramatic impact in the same city but represent very different church cultures and unique ministry models. Will's style blends the best of three worlds: process thinking from the discipline of engineering, communications savvy as an ad agency executive, and practical theology as a pastoral leader. His education includes a ThM in Pastoral Leadership from Dallas Theological Seminary and a B.S. in Chemical Engineering from Penn State. As you walk the vision pathway with Will, we invite you check-out his blog as an additional resource.

willmancini.com
twitter: willmancini
facebook.com/claritywill
instagram: will_be_clear

ACKNOWLEDGMENTS

I want to express special thanks to Cheryl Marting & Bob Adams. INNOVATING DISCIPLESHIP is a result of their collaboration and encouragement.

Finally, I want to thank all of the churches that allow me to come in and meddle with their models. Without you, I would not have the opportunity to learn and share with others. The gratitude I feel is perfectly captured in these words by Allan Karr and Linda Bergquist, "In some ways the most exquisite aspects of the design role are open only to the privileged. Just a few can design something new all of the time, and just a few have the luxury of doing so."

INNOVATING
DISCIPLESHIP

Four Paths to Real Discipleship Results